W9-DBC-757

SandCastle™

Baby
African Animals

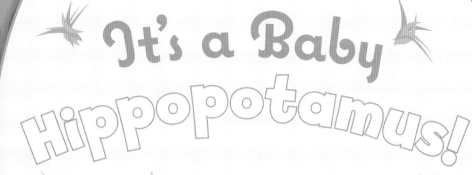

It's a Baby Hippopotamus!

Kelly Doudna

Consulting Editor, Diane Craig, M.A./Reading Specialist

ABDO
Publishing Company

Published by ABDO Publishing Company, 8000 West 78th Street, Edina, Minnesota 55439.

Printed in the United States.

Editor: Liz Salzmann
Content Developer: Nancy Tuminelly
Cover and Interior Design and Production: Mighty Media
Photo Credits: Digital Vision, iStockPhoto (Andy Didyk, Daniel Haller, Stephanie Kuwasaki), Peter Arnold Inc. (Mark Boulton, C. & M. Denis-Huot, TUNS, F. Vnoucek, P. Wegner)

Library of Congress Cataloging-in-Publication Data

Doudna, Kelly, 1963-
  It's a baby hippopotamus! / Kelly Doudna.
    p. cm. -- (Baby African animals)
  ISBN 978-1-60453-155-8
  1. Hippopotamus--Infancy--Juvenile literature. I. Title.

  QL737.U57D69 2009
  599.63'5139--dc22
                      2008007014

SandCastle™ Level: Fluent

SandCastle™ books are created by a team of professional educators, reading specialists, and content developers around five essential components—phonemic awareness, phonics, vocabulary, text comprehension, and fluency—to assist young readers as they develop reading skills and strategies and increase their general knowledge. All books are written, reviewed, and leveled for guided reading, early reading intervention, and Accelerated Reader® programs for use in shared, guided, and independent reading and writing activities to support a balanced approach to literacy instruction. The SandCastle™ series has four levels that correspond to early literacy development. The levels are provided to help teachers and parents select appropriate books for young readers.

| **Emerging Readers** | **Beginning Readers** | **Transitional Readers** | **Fluent Readers** |
| (no flags) | (1 flag) | (2 flags) | (3 flags) |

SandCastle™ would like to hear from you. Please send us your comments and suggestions.
sandcastle@abdopublishing.com

Vital Statistics

for the Hippopotamus

BABY NAME
calf

NUMBER IN LITTER
1

WEIGHT AT BIRTH
60 to 110 pounds

AGE OF INDEPENDENCE
6 to 8 years

ADULT WEIGHT
3,000 to 8,000 pounds

LIFE EXPECTANCY
40 years

Hippopotamus calves
are born on land or
underwater.

Calves can swim as soon
as they are born.

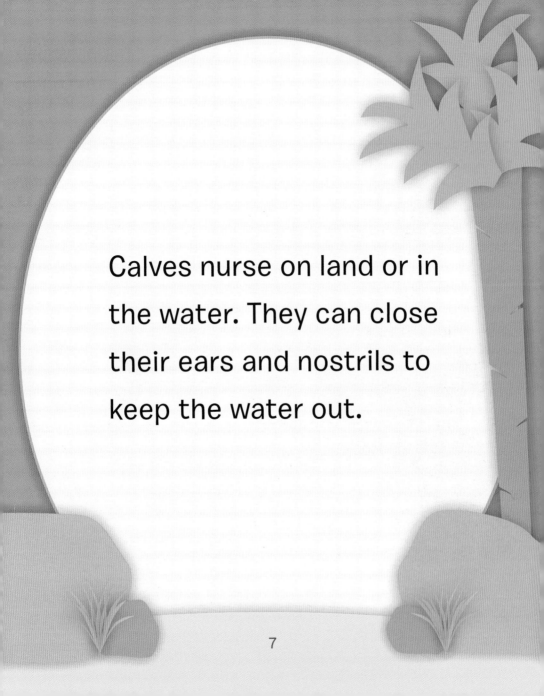

Calves nurse on land or in the water. They can close their ears and nostrils to keep the water out.

A group of hippos is called a pod.

Hippos stand in shallow water during the day. That is how they stay cool.

Hippos spend a lot of time underwater both awake and asleep. They must go to the surface every few minutes to breathe.

Hippos surface even while they are sleeping.

Hippos are very loud while they are in the water. They wheeze, grunt, bellow, and honk.

When one hippo starts making noise, other pod members join in!

Crocodiles are the main animal predator of hippos. They prey on hippo calves.

Hippos go onto land late in the day to eat grass. Adults can eat 80 pounds of grass in one night.

A mother hippo has one calf every two years. She might have several of her calves living with her at a time.

Fun Fact
About the Hippopotamus

A hippopotamus gives birth after only eight months. That's a short time compared to the elephant. An elephant gives birth after 22 months.

hippo = 8 months

elephant = 22 months

Glossary

expectancy – an expected or likely amount.

independence – no longer needing others to care for or support you.

nostril – an opening in the nose.

nurse – to feed a baby milk from the breast.

pod – a group of animals that are all one kind.

predator – an animal that hunts others.

prey – to hunt or catch an animal for food.

shallow – not deep.

surface – 1) the top of a body of water. 2) to rise or swim to the top of a body of water.

To see a complete list of SandCastle™ books and other nonfiction titles from ABDO Publishing Company, visit **www.abdopublishing.com**.

8000 West 78th Street, Edina, MN 55439

800-800-1312 • 952-831-1632 fax